Baton Twirling

by Julie Murray

ARTISTIC SPORTS

Abdo Kids

Abdo Kids Jumbo is an Imprint of Abdo Kids
abdobooks.com

abdobooks.com

Published by Abdo Kids, a division of ABDO, P.O. Box 398166, Minneapolis, Minnesota 55439. Copyright © 2023 by Abdo Consulting Group, Inc. International copyrights reserved in all countries. No part of this book may be reproduced in any form without written permission from the publisher. Abdo Kids Jumbo™ is a trademark and logo of Abdo Kids.

Printed in the United States of America, North Mankato, Minnesota.

102022
012023

Photo Credits: Alamy, AP Images, Getty Images, Shutterstock

Production Contributors: Teddy Borth, Jennie Forsberg, Grace Hansen
Design Contributors: Candice Keimig, Pakou Moua

Library of Congress Control Number: 2022937174
Publisher's Cataloging-in-Publication Data

Names: Murray, Julie, author.
Title: Baton twirling / by Julie Murray
Description: Minneapolis, Minnesota : Abdo Kids, 2023 | Series: Artistic sports | Includes online resources and index.
Identifiers: ISBN 9781098264208 (lib. bdg.) | ISBN 9781098264765 (ebook) | ISBN 9781098265045 (Read-to-Me ebook)
Subjects: LCSH: Baton twirling--Juvenile literature. | Sports--Juvenile literature. | Sports--History--Juvenile literature.
Classification: DDC 791.6--dc23

Table of Contents

Baton Twirling 4

Skills. 10

Batons & Costume 14

Competitions 18

More Facts 22

Glossary 23

Index 24

Abdo Kids Code. 24

Baton Twirling

Baton twirling is an exciting sport that uses a rod called a baton. The baton is used in a **coordinated** dance **routine**. Athletes move their bodies along with the baton.

Baton twirling became popular in the United States in the 1940s. It was performed in military parades. Twirlers spun rifles and **maces**.

Today, baton twirlers are often a part of marching bands. Many colleges have twirling teams too. It is also a worldwide **competitive** sport.

Skills

Baton twirling combines gymnastic and dance skills. Twirlers need to be **flexible**. They also must have good eye-hand coordination.

Twirlers perform a routine that is often choreographed to music. One or more batons can be used during a routine.

Batons & Costume

Most batons are made of lightweight metal. Weighted rubber is at each end. The larger end is called the ball. The smaller end is the tip.

Batons vary in length, thickness, and weight. Twirlers should have a baton that is the right size and fit for them. Twirlers also wear exciting costumes and jazz shoes or majorette boots.

Competitions

Baton twirling competitions are held around the world. Twirlers can perform **solo**. They can also compete in pairs or team competitions.

Competitions separate twirlers by age and skill level. The athletes are judged on skill, **routine** difficulty, and costumes. One of the most **competitive** titles is Miss **Majorette**. That title is given to the best baton twirler in each state.

21

More Facts

- The first World Baton Twirling Championships was held in Seattle, Washington, in 1980. Athletes from ten countries participated.

- ESPN hosts Twirl Mania each year at Walt Disney World in Orlando, Florida.

- The title of "Miss **Majorette** of America" is one of the highest baton twirling awards. It is earned by the top US twirler.

Glossary

choreograph – to plan the dance movements of a single dance, show, or the like, as in ballet or modern dance.

competitive – having to do with or decided by competition.

coordinated – to plan and cause two or more things to be the same or go together, as in movements along with music.

flexible – easily bent without breaking.

mace – a large ornamented tapered rod or baton used by a drum major to signal music and marching directions in a marching band or military band.

majorette – a woman or girl who leads a marching band and often twirls a baton.

routine – a worked-out part that may be often repeated.

solo – a performance by one person.

Index

awards 20

baton 4, 12, 14, 16

baton twirler 4, 8, 10, 16, 18, 20

college 8

competitions 18, 20

costumes 20

history 6

judging 20

marching band 8

materials 14

method 4

military parade 6

Miss Majorette 20

music 12

routine 4, 12, 20

teams 8, 18

Visit **abdokids.com** to access crafts, games, videos, and more!

Use Abdo Kids code **ABK4208** or scan this QR code!

24